Thoughts

Thoughts

ROBERT LEWIS SCHANKE

authorHOUSE®

AuthorHouse™
1663 Liberty Drive
Bloomington, IN 47403
www.authorhouse.com
Phone: 1-800-839-8640

Published by AuthorHouse   11/17/2012

ISBN: 978-1-4772-8239-7 (sc)
ISBN: 978-1-4772-8241-0 (hc)
ISBN: 978-1-4772-8237-3 (e)

Library of Congress Control Number: 2012919721

FOREWORD

THOUGHTS was written by Robert Schanke in his adult life.

Robert was born and raised in Minnesota where as a youth he was very active in scouting and recreation including running track. He was in the Navy three years during WWII and later attended Miami U. Ohio receiving a B.S. and M.S. in education degrees. Through out his life, he was very active in Boy Scouts. His interests included wood working, photography, camping and traveling.

He retired from education after 32 years, having taught math, science and recreation and later as an elementary principal.

THOUGHTS reflect his expressions of how he felt about various situations and individuals, what he observed and what he recalled from his youth and days in the past. THOUGHTS came to him at various times—while at school—while at home with his family—while traveling in the United States and abroad.

During his retirement he has gathered together his THOUGHTS to publish for others to enjoy.

INTRODUCTION

A book
Is like a pantry
For the mind.

Words
Are
Words
Are
Just Words.

But words
Give life
To
Our thoughts.

Contents

CHAPTER ONE

A Gift of Love

CHAPTER TWO

Children . . . What a Blessing

CHAPTER THREE

Family . . . Makes this house a Home

CHAPTER FOUR

Feelings from the Heart

CHAPTER ONE

A Gift of Love

A GIFT

I give to you
The only gift I have.
A gift which one can not see
But one can feel.
A gift which costs little
And yet is priceless.
A gift which everyone
Is not willing to give.
Someday you will know
What I give to you alone . . . .

rls

TOGETHER

I had looked forward
To the coming
Of the day,
Enjoyed
The short time together
And
Look back
With beautiful thoughts . . .

rls

WHEN IT COMES

We don't know
When,
We don't know
How,
We don't know
Why,
But it comes.
It is called love.

Love comes
In different sizes
And
In different ways.
But,
It comes . . .

rb

SOME WORDS

Some words
Are
Just words.
They take up space
And
Take Time.
Other words
Have meaning
Because
They come
From the mind
And
From the heart.

rls

THREE WISHES

If I had but three wishes,
The first would be for you,
The second would be for happiness,
The third,
That the first two
Would come true . . .

rb

TOUCH

There is nothing
As beautiful
As love,
For it is
A touch of God
Upon the heart . . . .

rb

I Love You

There is nothing material
Which I can give
That you don't already have.

There is nothing new
Which I can give
That I haven't already given.

I can only continue to give
My love and trust
And tell you that I will be near
Whenever you need me.

For I love you . . . .

rls

Robert Lewis Schanke

I Need You

Can you but tell me that you love me,
Not because I ask this of you,
But because you want me to know.

Can you but say that you are proud
Of my work knowing that I do it
Because of your encouragement.

Will you but touch my cheek
With your lips without my asking,
To tell me that you approve of my being.

Will you but come to me because
You want me and not because
I need you . . .

rb

A LOVE STORY

One word,
One touch,
One look,
One love . . .

rls

LOVE

Love doesn't come
In big chunks.
It can be felt,
But not seen.
It can be given,
But not taken.
It can be demonstrated
In many small ways . . .

rls

ROSES

Red roses
May be given
A dozen at a time
Or
One at a time
As away of giving
A sincere Compliment
Or for just
Being there when needed . . .

Special Moment

For a moment
I thought
I was alone
In the house.
Then I heard
An almost silent click,
A door being opened?
Was it a door?
Or
A heart that just said
Yes?

rls

NOW

Until now,
I thought
The sun shown
Everyday.

I wasn't the wiser
Until a friend
Pointed out
The grayness
Of now . . . .

rb

Yes,
The sun is
Always shining,
It's just that
Sometimes
We can't see it . . .

rb

A smile

Starts

In the heart.

Sometimes

We even allow it

To show

On our face . . . .

rls

See
With your eyes
But
Listen
With your heart . . .

rls

If
You really want
To know a person,
Listen
To what their eyes
Are saying.

rls

CHAPTER TWO

Children . . .
What a Blessing

CHILDREN

Children
Are the expression
Of
His faith
In Mankind.

We choose
To work with
Children.
And are privileged,
For so many
Little children
Need what
So few can give.

So many
Little children
Are
The composite
Of
So many things.

Things over which
We or they
Have little control.

Are
We the answer . . . . ?

rb

OUR LIVES

Children are not a sacrifice,
They are a blessing.
Without them
We would find other ways
To spend our
Time,
Energies,
And money.

With them
This is unnecessary.
For our children
Become our lives
And
For a time
We are theirs . . .

rls

LISTEN TO THEM

Today,
I met with a young lady.
She came to me
Almost ready to cry
Because of what she thought
Was a failure.
The only failure was
In not allowing a child
To be a child.

Children
Are little people,
Having the same desires,
Needs and emotions
As
Big people.

Like most people
They want what they want
When they want it.
We fail to realize
That
If we always expect them
To do as we direct,
We are as stubborn
As they.

Sometimes
We must remember
What childhood is like.
To know that
A lasting learning situation
Does not develop
When we are always told
What to do.
We must involve ourselves
In a child's learning experience.
We must be enthused
About children.

We must remember
That
Sometimes they are
A bundle of nerves
Wrapped in a pink cotton dress.
That the desire to be active
Outweighs the desire
To be quiet.
That the desire to create
Is more important
Than the desire
To mind . . . .

rls

FAITH

Children are children.
Learn to
Live with them,
Love them,
Enjoy them,
But
Most of all,
Have faith in them
And
In yourself as a teacher.

rls

LEAVES

The leaves were blown
Across the
School yard
As if someone
Had just rung the bell
Ending recess.

rls

COMMUNICATE

Strange
How we spend years
Teaching others
To recognize shapes,
Colors,
Letters,
Words.
Teach them
To
Sing,
Dance,
Ride,
Play,
Paint,
And to express
Themselves
In every way
And
Then as adults
We don't let them.

HONEST I AM

I like to
Fold and paste
Teacher.
It's fun.
The paste smells
So good.
It's kinda sticky too.

I didn't mean to
Push it
On the floor
Teacher,
Really I didn't.

Take my paper
In my
Left hand?
The long way?
This way?
Which side teacher?
Teacher, which hand
Is my
Left hand?
Fold the right side
To The left?
But,
I thought it was
All the way to the left.
Teacher, please
Don't go so fast . . .

I'm just
A little guy
And can do
Just little
Things.
Teacher,
Please don't get
Angry.
I'm trying,
Honest I am.

Why do you
Help
All the others
And
And you just scold me?
Really,
I like to
Fold and paste
But I can't
Do it good.

Wait for me
Teacher.
Please,
I'm just a
Little guy.

I want to be
As good
As the rest
But
Sometimes

A little kid
Inside of me
Does other things
Like pushing
Things off
My desk
When I know
I shouldn't
And like
Laughing and talking
Too loud
When I know
You want me to be
Quiet.

Honest teacher,
I try.
Please don't be
Angry with me
Like my
Mommy and daddy
Sometimes are.

I'm trying teacher,
Honest
I am . . . .

WORTH SOMETHING

Hey teacher,
How come
You always talk to me
As a kid?
It sounds like
You feel you're
Better than me.
You make me feel
Like I'm not
Worth anything.

Why don't you
Talk to me
As a people
And make me feel
I'm important
Too.

I need to know
I'm worth
Something . . . .

rls

I Hurt Inside

Thank you
For trying
To understand me.
I can't always
Let people know
How I feel or
What I want to say.
It is difficult
To have so much
Inside me
When
I don't know
How to get it out.
I hurt,
My head hurts.
I want to be
Like the rest,
But somehow I can't.
I'm not like
The other kids.
What made me different?
Is it my fault?
Thank you
For being here
When I need
To be held,

When I need
To be taken
From the group
Because
Of my frustrations.
Thank you
For being firm
But yet
Gentle.
My screaming
And kicking are
The only ways
I can relieve
My torment.
I'm angry
With no one
But myself.
It's difficult
Being six
Feeling the way I do.
Will I ever
Be seven?

FIRST GRADER

Mommy,
Ya gotta come to school
Tomorrow at 9:30
Teacher said so.
No,
I wasn't bad.
We have to put on a play.
You'll like it mom,
I'm a duck.
Hey mom,
You're not listening
To me.
Ya gotta come.
Here's the note
From my teacher.
Hey, you didn't read it.
Mommy,
Why don't you listen
To me like my teacher does?
Don't you like me
Anymore?

rb

First Friend

Mom
Hey mommy
There's someone
At the door.
Can I
Let her in?

Hi,
Moms here
I'll get her.
Mom come here.

She talks nice.
She's a teacher?
My new teacher?

Tell her
About me,
Mommy,
Tell her about me.
You know mom,
I think
I'm going to
Like school
This year.

Mommy where's
My daddy?

CHAPTER THREE

Family . . .
Makes this house
a Home

MY HAND IS THERE

We talk
But
As we do,
I see something missing.

It changes.
The sparkle
In her eyes
Isn't always there.
Not like it used to be.
I notice also,
Her voice sometimes
Isn't as bright
As it used to be.

These changes aren't always evident
But just often enough
To be noticed.
I wonder why or what
Has caused this.
Is there anyway
I can understand?
Is there anything
A father can do?

I think I know why
And I am here.
My hand is always out to her.
She will take it
When she needs it.

OUR FAMILY

This
Is our first Thanksgiving
Apart from
One another.

It is a way
Of acknowledging
Our individual
Independence.

We have been
A close family
Yet
One which recognizes
The importance of
Each member.

Your mother
And I feel
We have had
More than our share
Of beautiful moments
With both of you.

You will always
Have our
Love,
Admiration,
And respect . . . .

BE THE MAN YOU WILL BE

I stand at the door
As you leave.
Not knowing
When
I'll see you again.

Our life together
Has been
A friendship,
A time
Of two people
Growing
Together.

The time
For growing apart
Will come.

Soon you will be
On your own.
Your life experiences
Will be controlled
By you.

Use the past
As a guide
For the days
Ahead.

Change
What needs changing.

Hold fast
To that which you can accept.

Be the man
You will be . . . .

rls

Don't grow up
Too fast
You'll be old
Long enough
Anyway.

rls

Don't
Ever pretend
You are someone
You are not.

rls

Don't worry about me,
But don't
You ever forget your mother.

rls

LISTEN

Years ago
I asked that
You listen to everyone.
Take from each
The wisdom
You can use.
Leave the rest.
One other thought
Follows that.
Find out
What part you play
In the society.
Find your own space
As it relates
To others.
Be willing
To defend your beliefs,
But
Don't for a minute

Believe
You can convince
Others to think
As you do.
Listen to them,
But don't always accept
Their ideas as
Being absolute.
Learn to question,
But trust.
Learn to listen,
And believe.
Be willing
To accept the change
That you will
Experience
Within yourself . . .

A LITTLE RED LEAF

Years ago,
In fact it was December 1945,
I was stationed aboard
A small navy ship in the Philippines.
One day
A rather fat letter arrived
From mom and dad.
It contained a 3" piece
Of their Minnesota Christmas tree.
What a welcome scent
It brought from home.
A home I hadn't seen
For about a year.
A mom, dad and sister I missed.

Time passes,
Some memories fade,
But one day much later
I found a small
But beautiful red leaf
In our yard.

It brought back the Christmas
Of many years earlier,
A Christmas far from home.
I enclosed the little read leaf
In my next letter home.
I hope they remembered.

I was returning their love
From many years earlier.
When I needed "a little bit of home."

rls

Almost Completed

How long
It has been
Since
A little girl
Sat beside me
And we talked.

Talked
Of the things
Fathers and daughters
Talk about.
About things,
About people,
And
About being
The best person
It's possible
To be.

She's still
My little girl
And I love her.
But loving
Means
Allowing to grow,
Allowing to stand
On her own
Two feet,
Respecting her judgment.
She is capable
In every way.

My work with her
Is almost complete.
Now I can
Be in the background
Of her life
And
Be completely happy
With her . . .

rls

LITTLE ONE

One of these days
I may have
Another
Young lady
Sitting beside me.
She'll be like
Her mom
In many ways.
She'll be quite,
She'll listen,
And when the time comes
She too, will be
Strong,
Forming her judgments
With compassion
And wisdom.

DAD

Not long ago
We found ourselves
Listening
To the Cincinnati Pops
Orchestra.
As they played
The Overture
To Die Fledermaus
I remembered
Dad.
On a Sunday afternoon,
Listening to
The same music.
He would put aside
What
He was reading,
Close his eyes
And
I am sure
Felt he was
Front row center.

Suddenly
Thousands of people
Around me
Were no longer there.
I was alone
And the music
Was played
Just for me.
At the end
Of the music
I realized
I was again
Part of the thousands
Enjoying Strauss.
But
For a moment
I remembered
Dad's love
For music
And
Dad . . .

Our Little Girl

Mom and dad
I like
Being with you.
I like
Your smiles.
I'm just a little girl
And sometimes
I don't know
How to say a word.

I was telling grandpa
About a story
And
He didn't understand
The word I used.

You helped him
Know I wanted
To say 'st' and
It only came out a 't'
When you told him
This,
My face felt sad
And
I backed away
From you.

In a little while
I felt better
And sat
On my small tractor,
Played with a game
And my ball.

Grandpa came over
And tickled me
And I fell off
My ball and tractor
And you smiled.
I felt good
Because you
Smiled again.
I like your smiles.

LITTLE RED WAGON

As a young girl
She shared
Her Little Red Wagon
With her sister.

Many years later
We pulled
Our daughter
Along
The country road
Near where
We lived,
And later
Her brother
Enjoyed the same
Little Red Wagon.

Now
Sixty-five years old
The Little Red Wagon
Has become
Part of our landscape.

Many happy memories
Are remembered
Each time we see it . . .

rls

US

Know what else
Sundays are for?

I'm alone now
But
I'd like to
Take a walk
With a friend.

A quiet walk
For I learned
From my dad
That words aren't
Always necessary.
Just the presence
Of a friend.

Want to?

A Narrow gravel road
Leading past a few
Small tired homes and through a
Quiet countryside.

Smiles on our faces
And minds.
Only good thoughts
About the beauty
Around us.

Past trees which
Covered their feet
With their leaves.

Spring birds
Adding life to
The still naked woods.

Thoughts pass
Between us.
Agreeable thoughts.

I see her smiling eyes
But,
I see something
Deeper.
Something not family
Related,
But a secret
She holds but doesn't
Want to.

GRANDPA'S FARM

Grandpa's farm
And tall pine trees
Along the drive.
No grass but
Brown pine needles
Beneath.
Small boy and girl
Riding broomstick horses.

Night wind
In the pines.
Scary sounds.
Owls.
Strange bedroom.
Oatmeal breakfasts.
Ticking clock on
Nearby shelf.
Wood range,
Oil stove,
Rocking chair
Near screened
Door.

Gingerbread porch,
Lilacs,
Pump,
Wooden watering tank,
Cows,
Woodshed,
Hollyhocks,
Goodbyes,
Down circle drive
And
Back to our home.

rls

BEING TWELVE

Sunday morning
Church bells
In the distance.
Back when
I was about twelve,
I remember
Being on the farm
And hearing them.
The carefree,
Innocent days
Of childhood.
Carefree and innocent
Now,
But full of
Being twelve
Problems
Then.
The quietness
Of the morning,
The time to think
With a twelve year old
Mind.

Not really knowing
What or
How to
Think.
Not really having
Answers
For
Many things
But
Still caught up
In life and
All the strange
Things
That happen
To
A twelve year old . . . .

rls

MY FIRST DIME

A young boy
Climbing a hill.
Small bucket
Of water in
Hand.
Grandpa and neighbors
Planting tobacco.
Hot,
Tired,
Thirsty.
Horse pulling
Tobacco planter.
Grandpa
Stops the horse,
Takes the bucket
And places
In the boy's small hand
A bright dime.
A happy boy
Skipping back
To the farmhouse.

rb

PLEASE

Allow my son to be an individual,
Don't make him one.

Allow him to be unique,
Don't make him unique.

Allow him to be different,
Don't make him different.

Help him to understand.
Respect for
God,
Country,
Others,
And for himself.
Without the latter
He will not know the others.

Teach him to know
Honesty,
Beauty,
And compassion.
Teach him to be
Sensitive and
Humble,
But not to sell himself short.

If you will teach him
These things,
He will become
A man worth knowing.

rb

SON

I guess I don't
Call you that
Very often.

As a young man
I told you several times
That I was proud of you
And you often
Asked me why.

I'll try again
To let you know.

I'm proud of
For who you are,
For what you are,
For your wholesome beliefs
And
For what you are doing
With your life.

Mom and I
Couldn't have a finer son
And we want you to know,
We love you, Terry.

rls

GROWING UP

You're already ten, Josh
I'm thinking
Of all the great times
We've shared
Over those years.
The farm pond,
Cows,
Tractor rides,
Haying,
Biking the lane
And more . . . .
I've enjoyed
Being with you
All these years.
As I watched you grow,
I like what I see
In you.
I'm proud of you
And what you can do.

As you grow,
You'll experience
Many things,
Many good and
Beautiful things.
Some not so good
And you will have to
Make a decision.
Not all decisions
Are easy.
Do what you know
Is right
And
In all respects,
Play the game
By the rules . . .

rls

A Gentle Hand

I remember
Years ago
When you were
About six or seven,
We were camping
With others.
A hike took us
Several miles
From camp
And
Every mile
You filled your pockets
With shiny stones.
The miles
Took their toll though,
For you became
A tired little fella.

A friend placed you
On his shoulders
And carried you
Several miles
Back to camp.
You were borne
On the shoulders
Of another
When you needed it.

You too
Have your turn.
It may be
A student,
A teacher,
A friend.
Don't carry too soon
For people will expect it.
Don't wait too long
For hopes of success
Disappear.

You are a man.
Stand tall
Be there
When you are needed,
For the tired
Welcome
A gentle hand.

LOVE AND RESPECT

Where
Did all the years
Go?

Remember
The red and white jump seat
Worn out
By an active
Son.

Remember
Burr haircuts,
Scouting,
Hiking,
Camping.

The
"Follow me"
At age five
In
Cypress Gardens.

The Pinewood Derby
Racer
I still keep
Along
With his black and white
Teddy bear.

The
Track,
Wrestling,
Football,
Band,
Days at high school.

That first
Blue car
And
Several others
And
All the things
That went wrong
With them.

The
"I'm going to college
For an
Education"
To the radio
Announcer during
A high school football game.

That first day
At college and
The long trip home
For
Mom and Dad.

There were
Those lonesome days
For him as well.

The discouragement
Of not knowing

What comes next
In life.

The camaraderie
With
The great college roommates.
The understanding
Which comes
From
An understanding heart.

The pride of standing
On your own two feet.
The new experiences
Gained
With new responsibility.

And
The knowledge
That
In the background
There will always be
People
Who love
And
Respect you . . .

CHAPTER FOUR

Feelings from the Heart

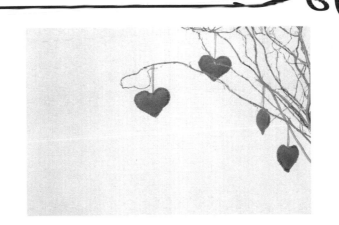

WHATEVER

Whatever you start,
Finish.

Whatever you do,
Do your best.

This above all,
Play the game
By the rules . . . .

TALKING

After talking
With a friend,
I remembered
What he said
And
What I said.
I wish
I could remember what
I should have said.

rb—

RULES

I've always tried
To play the game
By the rules.
Even
Setting the rules
At times.
I expect others
To do the same.
Sometimes
When I am forced
To play by the rules
I don't like them . . . .

rls

WHAT MORE

Sunny fall days,
Leaves falling,
Ground covered,
Stillness in the air
And
Gladness
In the heart.
But thoughts
Of us
Are elsewhere.
We are here
Together.
What more can
One ask?

LITTLE YELLOW CROCUS

Remember
The little yellow crocus
Slowly pushing its way up
Through the frost.

Think
Of the small stream.
Listen to it,
And the delicate sounds
Of its movement.
Not knowing
Where it starts,
Not knowing
Where it will end,
But knowing
It will continue to flow
Until it becomes
Part of something larger.

Remember
The sound of footsteps
On a leaf covered trail.
The crisp sound of your steps,
Your kicking leaves
Into the air to see
How far they will go.

Think
Of the first wet snow,
The laughter of
Your first snowball,
The many tracks
You leave behind
In making
Your first snowman,
The cold snow
Down your back,
The warmth of the kitchen
As you end your winter day.

Think again
Of the little yellow crocus.
It will come again
And
You'll be anxious
For its return.
Remember
The beauty
Of your life . . .

LIFE

What happened
To the rainbows?
Don't they make them
Anymore?
Where did the flowers
And the raindrops go?

Time was for bare feet
In the grass,
For roller-skating
And
For wooden whistles.
Are they still here
And I don't see them?
Have the years
Changed my thoughts
About important things?

Make the Most

Walk tall.
Hold your head high.
You will become
What you will.
No one
Can walk tall
For you.
No one can
Hold their head high
For you.

Shape your life
From your good
Experiences.
Use your failures
As stepping stones.
Accept yourself
As you are.
For you will become
What you want
To be . . . .

A SPECIAL GIFT

Everyone has a gift.
Some don't even know it.
Just listen
To your special voice
And
You will know
What it is.
Listen, it is there.
Your special gift.

rls

FEELING GOOD

You
Have the talent
For
Always making me
Feel good
About myself . . . .

rb

TOMORROWS
ARE NEVER THE SAME
AS YESTERDAYS

SOMETIMES WE TALK
WITHOUT THINKING
AND
SOMETIMES WE THINK
WITHOUT TALKING

rb

There are no
Cloudy days
Only days
That appear
Cloudy . . .

rb

EYES

Watch their eyes
For the eyes
Bypass the mouth
And come directly
From the heart.

rls

A good diet
Is to
Eat right
Exercise right
And
Think right . . .

rls

ORGANIZATION

Is knowing
What to do,
How to do it,
When to do it
And then,
Getting it done . . .

rb

Every question
Has an answer.
It's just that sometimes
We don't like
The answer . . .

rb

REMEMBER

Hang onto beautiful moments
And live them many times.
Too often we expect
Every moment to be beautiful.

Too often we're disappointed
With our life
For we don't look for
The pleasant experiences
But see only life as it appears
To be—ordinary.

Without the rain
The sunshine has no meaning.
Without the night, the day.
Without a hurt, a touch.
Without a tear, a smile.

Look back to one thing
Which made you happy yesterday.
Relive it, remember it
And hang onto the memory
For a lifetime.
It is yours . . . .

rls

PEOPLE

Some people look
But do not see.
Some people hear
But do not listen.
Some people . . . .

rb

Think
HAPPY THOUGHTS

rb

Thursdays
Are
FOR THINKING.

rb

BE STRONG

Don't
Let anyone
Talk you
Into doing something
Which makes you
Feel uncomfortable
Or
For which
You don't feel ready.

rls

I WAS JUST THINKING,
We see what we want to see,
We hear what we want to hear,
We believe what we want to believe.
And yet,
We search endlessly to find support
For our beliefs . . .

rls

CHILDREN'S CORNER

The father of a newborn, touched by wonder, ponders what lies ahead for the small child in his arms. Such was the inspiration for Rudyard Kipling's "If," a verse extolling wisdom, patience and other fine and virtuous qualities; after several stanzas, the poet proclaims, "Yours is the Earth and everything that's in it."

Tuesday, June 27

Remember
There are some things
In life
YOU DON'T HAVE TO DO . . . .

rb

Do right
Because
It is right
And not because
You expect
Something in return.

rb

Tell me,
Do I look
As old as I feel
Or
Do I just feel
As old as I look?

rb

Your List

Make sure
That your
"I wish I had" list
Is longer
Than your
"I wish I hadn't" list.

rls

Forgive

Forgiveness may
Be given.
Forgiveness may
Be received.
But
May one ask
For forgiveness?

rls

LIVE

We all have
To live with
Our past
But
How much baggage
We carry with us
Is our problem.

rb

TIME

Sometimes in life
A few moments
Seem like hours
And
At other times
An hour seems
Like a few minutes.
Which is it?

rb

TEARS

Tears come
At strange times.
Not when
We expect them
But
When they are
Really needed.
Not from a physical hurt
But
From a beautiful thought,
A beautiful sight
Or a beautiful memory.
There must be
A reason for this.
Do we know why?
Should we know why?

DESPAIR

The warm tears
Of despair
Slowly fill my eyes.
Move down
My cheeks,
And fall silently
From my face . . . .

rb

REALITY

GOD,
The world is complex.
Everyone
Is trying to solve problems.
Some aren't even theirs.
People look to others
To help them know
A perfect life.

Many
Don't believe
That some things
Can be resolved
Within,
With time and faith.

So many
Want the answer now.
Do we have to
Make a decision
About the rest
Of our life
As though
Once we did
We wouldn't change.

There are many
Roads to follow.
I'd like to
Follow them,
But not alone.

I need someone
To follow them
With me.

I must be
A dreamer.

Reality
Confronts us all
And can take from us
The beauty
Of life,
The compassion
For every living thing.

Reality can keep us
From knowing
Each other.
It leads us blindly
To follow rules,
To be images
Of people
And
To keep us
From knowing ourselves
And from loving others.

PACIFIC COAST

Rusty, tired
Windmills
Standing where once
A home site stood.
Dark, heavy
Sky.
No sound.
No life.

Suddenly I see
Nodding sunflower
Faces
In the flatlands
Of the Midwest.
Sky bright,
Clouds light,
Peace.

Then my thoughts
Turn to children.
Round,
Smiling faces,
Bright eyes,
The world comes alive
With them.

Round windmills,
Round sunflowers,
Round faces,
Life . . . .

DANDELION JUNGLE

Rain
Causing
Naked dandelions
To jump,
Their white hair
Falling
To replenish
Their kind
On
Another day.

People
Whacking,
Digging and
Cutting
The dandelion jungle,
Trying to reduce
It
To nothingness.
Depriving the
Birds of food,
Little children
Of first bouquets
For mothers
And
Teachers
And
The lawn
Of ugliness . . . .

MY WORDS

The words which come
From my pen
Are my words.
They come from
My heart.

The words which come
From my mouth
Are also my words
But
Sometimes they bypass
My heart and head.

I want them
To be more
But
With some people
I find it to be difficult.

I know why
This is,
But do they?

rb

WORDS
Are
Words
Are
Just words
But words
Give life
To
Our thoughts
Now think about it.

rb